T0347458

LIVE Your Own WILD LiFE

A JOURNAL FOR HUMANS WITH ADVICE FROM ANIMALS

by CATHERINE LEPAGE

CHRONICLE BOOKS

SAN FRANCISCO

Text and illustrations copyright © 2019 by Catherine Lepage.
All rights reserved. No part of this product may be reproduced in
any form without written permission from the publisher.

ISBN 978-1-4521-7158-6

Manufactured in China

10 9 8 7 6 5 4 3 2 1

Chronicle Books publishes distinctive books and gifts. From
award-winning children's titles, bestselling cookbooks, and
eclectic pop culture to acclaimed works of art and design,
stationery, and journals, we craft publishing that's instantly
recognizable for its spirit and creativity. Enjoy our publishing
and become part of our community at www.chroniclebooks.com.

Special quantity discounts are available to corporations and
other organizations. Contact our premiums department at
corporatesales@chroniclebooks.com or at 1-800-759-0190.

Chronicle Books LLC
680 Second Street
San Francisco, California 94107
www.chroniclebooks.com

For Simon, Léo, Madeleine, and Yvonne,
the very best Wild Life partners.

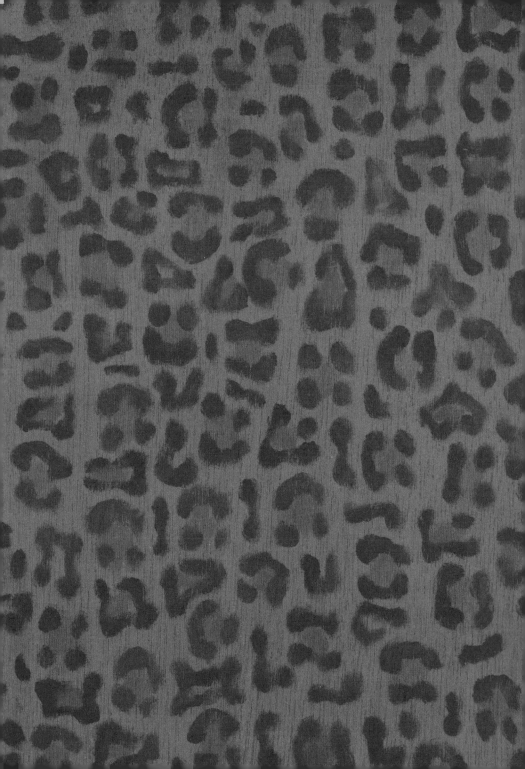

Know how your brain works and use it in your favor.

This is a thought.

This is your brain.

*We cannot always
control our thoughts.*

But our thoughts tend to follow the same paths
over and over again. The more they use a trail,
the wider it gets and the easier it is to follow.
And the easier it is to follow, the more they will
be tempted to use this trail.

You don't like where your thoughts take you?

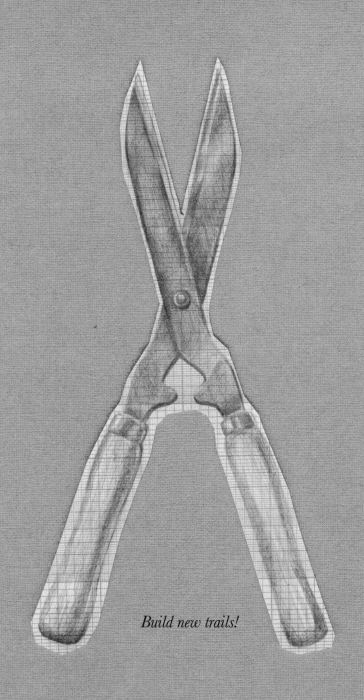

Build new trails!

*The more you visualize where you want to be emotionally,
the more the trails that will get you there will open up, and
your thoughts will start using the new trails naturally.*

*Forget about the negative trails; if you don't send your thoughts
down them, they will become overgrown and disappear with time.*

*Now, let this journal guide you through the wilderness,
and build your dream trails!*

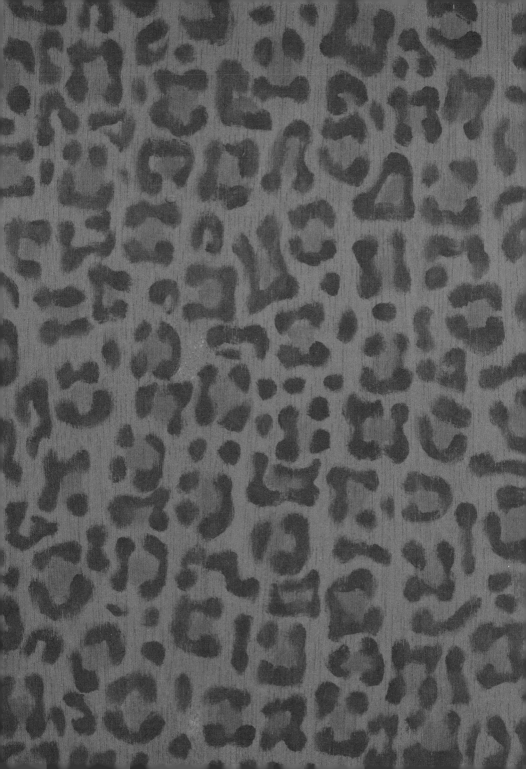

Take the
"How is your
life going?"
test:

DO YOU TOLERATE SITUATIONS THAT YOU DON'T LIKE?

☐ All the time

☐ Sometimes

☐ Never

DO YOU HAVE RACING THOUGHTS THAT WON'T SLOW DOWN?

☐ All the time

☐ Sometimes

☐ Never

DO YOU COMPARE YOURSELF TO OTHERS?

☐ All the time   ☐ Sometimes   ☐ Never

DO YOU WAIT FOR OTHERS TO FULFILL YOUR NEEDS?

☐ All the time

☐ Sometimes

☐ Never

ARE YOU FOCUSING ON THINGS YOU CAN'T HAVE?

☐ All the time

☐ Sometimes

☐ Never

DO YOU LIVE THROUGH OTHER PEOPLE'S EYES?

☐ All the time

☐ Sometimes

☐ Never

DO YOU AVOID LISTENING TO CRITICS?

☐ All the time

☐ Sometimes

☐ Never

DO YOU SPLIT YOUR ENERGY IN OPPOSITE DIRECTIONS?

☐ All the time   ☐ Sometimes   ☐ Never

QUESTION 9

DO YOU TRY TO HIDE WHAT MAKES YOU DIFFERENT?

☐ All the time   ☐ Sometimes   ☐ Never

RESULTS:

If you answered
"ALL THE TIME"
or
"SOMETIMES"
at least once:

You can certainly make your life
happier, more fulfilling, and more
serene, one goal at a time.

If you answered
"NEVER"
to all questions:

You are a really lucky and well-balanced person!

HOW TO START:

Stick a Post-it on the pages where you
answered "all the time" or "sometimes," and on it
write down one thing you can change to improve
your life in this area. When you're done, you
will have a beautiful list of goals.

Chose one goal from the list. Find one word that will
remind you of that goal. Write this word on many
Post-its and stick them up all around you—on your
mirror, in your car, in the fridge. . . . You need to
see this word often! When you reach your goal, write
it down on the "Success" page at the end of this
journal, and start again with your next goal.

GOOD NEWS!

You can do this quiz over and over until you can proudly
and sincerely answer "never" to all the questions.

In the meantime, use this journal to chart your progress,
reflect on your experience, and brainstorm new goals.

To blaze a trail toward your goal, you'll need to:

Know what you WANT
TO CHANGE! Don't try to
fight several battles at the same time;
focus on one goal at a time.

Make a
STEP - BY - STEP plan
and stick to it!

HUNT DOWN YOUR FEARS.

and FACE THEM.

Work ON YOUR WEAKNESSES.

LEAP *Outside* YOUR COMFORT ZONE.

WORK ON YOUR SORE POINTS

Some more...

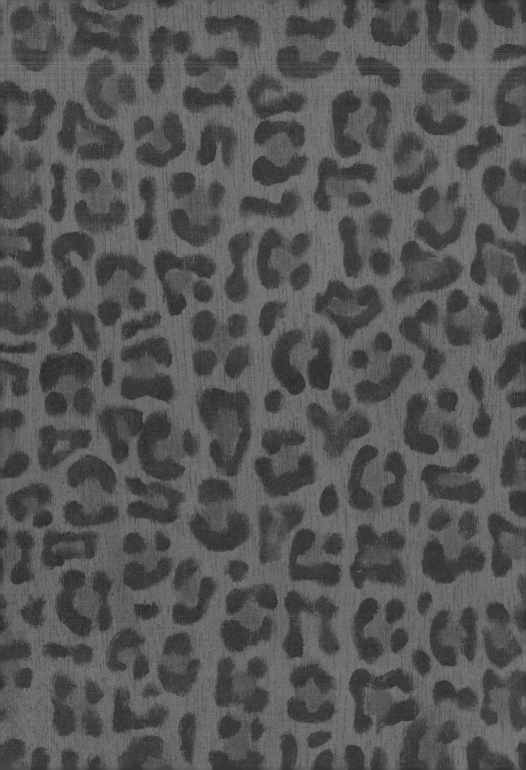

Weeds and stray branches may block your path. . . .

Things might not change
AS FAST AS YOU'D LIKE.
But do a little every day
and you'll go a long way!

SOMETIMES things are unfair.

COMPLAINING won't help, so USE THESE
EXPERIENCES to learn **HOW**
you can create a better outcome next time.

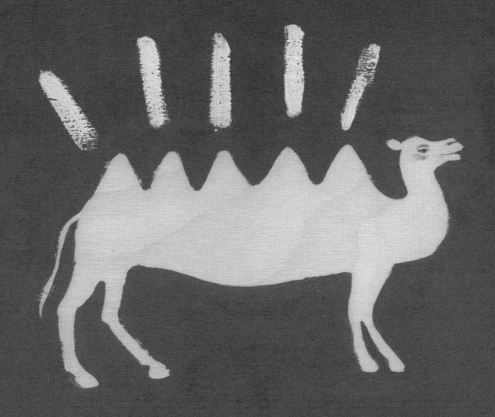

Remember life is full of UPS and DOWNS. AT SOME POINT, YOU'LL THINK ABOUT GIVING UP. Allow yourself a break, and then continue working on your goals the next day!

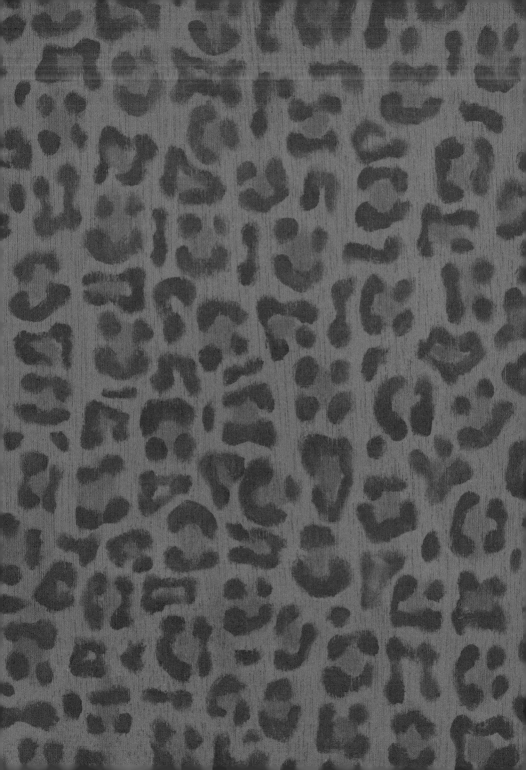

Wisdom from off the beaten path:

YOU HAVE THE RIGHT

TO Choose your own way.

DON'T PRETEND TO BE

someone you're _not_.

What works FOR OTHERS
MIGHT NOT WORK for you.

Know your limits,
AND STAY AWAY
FROM WHAT HARMS YOU.

Trust your instincts.
IF THEY SAY "DON'T GO", DON'T.

Focus on peace;

IT WILL CHASE AWAY
NEGATIVE THOUGHTS.

Being fragile is NOT A CRIME.
ACCEPT YOUR VULNERABILITY.
FRAGILITY IS NOT WEAKNESS.

Tips to
lighten the
load :

BALANCE WORK

AND PLAY.

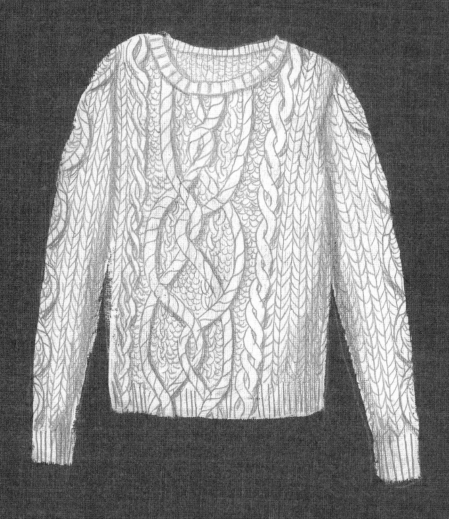

PURSUE PROJECTS

THAT MAKE YOU FEEL USEFUL.

SURROUND YOURSELF WITH
THINGS YOU LIKE.

BUT DON'T BECOME A SLAVE
TO YOUR POSSESSIONS.

GET RID OF WHAT
YOU DON'T REALLY NEED.

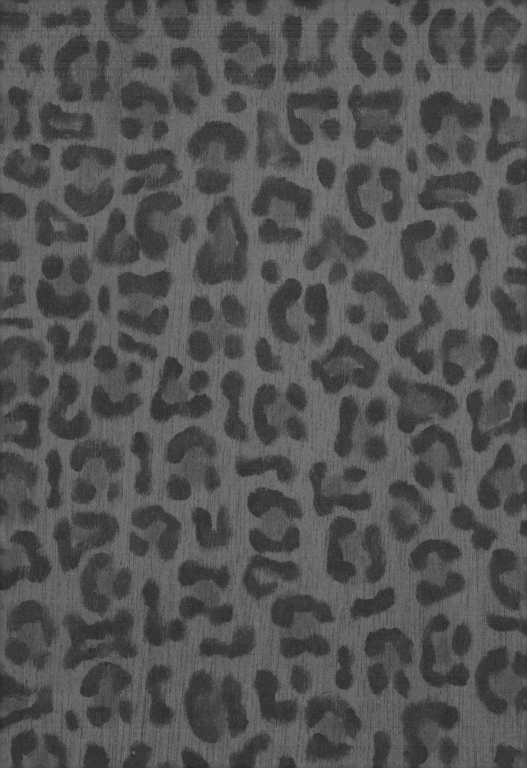

Don't forget
to enjoy
the scenery
along the way.

A GOOD MOOD is
contagious.
SURROUND YOURSELF
WITH POSITIVE PEOPLE.

Getting old DOESN'T MEAN
YOU HAVE TO TAKE YOURSELF
seriously.

PROBLEMS FEEL <u>LIGHTER</u>
WHEN YOU
share THE load.

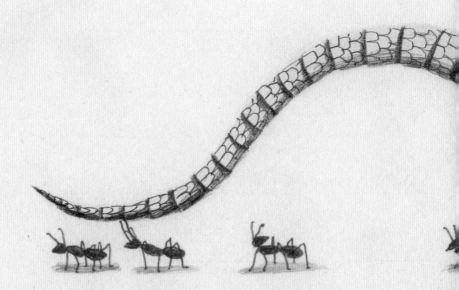

DON'T POISON
YOURSELF
WITH RESENTMENT. Forgive.

AND MOST OF ALL...

Keep going !

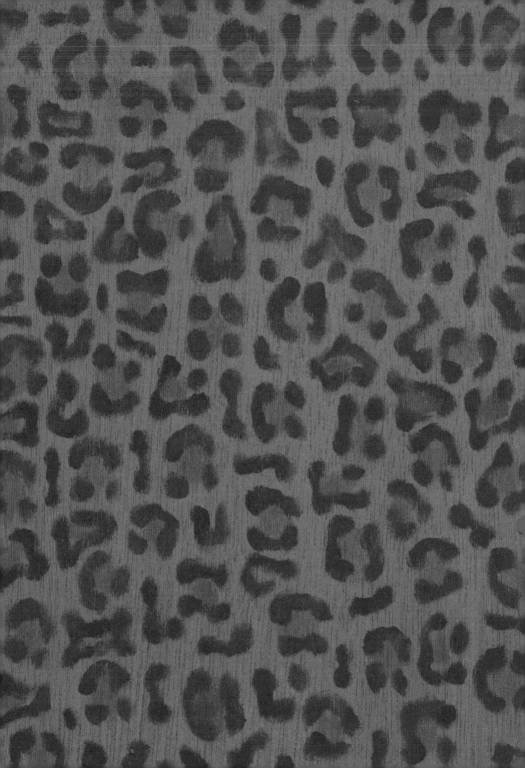

Your own
wild
toolbox

LIST ALL THE WAYS IN WHICH YOU ARE UNIQUE.

WRITE ABOUT SOME EXPERIENCES WHEN YOU WERE ABLE TO BEAT THE ODDS.

BRAINSTORM WAYS
TO ESCAPE YOUR ROUTINE
ONCE IN A WHILE.

WHAT ARE THE TECHNIQUES YOU USE WHEN YOU'RE FACING A DIFFICULTY?

WHEN YOU'RE FEELING BAD, SOMETIMES IT'S HARD TO REMEMBER IT WON'T LAST FOREVER.

Write yourself some reminders here.

THERE'S NO LIMIT
TO YOUR DREAMS!

Write them down and read them often.

THE **SUCCESS** PAGE

YOU HAVE THE ABILITY TO CHANGE!

Use the next few pages to celebrate
the goals you've already attained.